SAUDADE
SORROW

Poems by
Claribel Alegría

Translated by
Carolyn Forché

CURBSTONE PRESS

First printing: September, 1999. Second printing: May, 2000.

Printed on acid-free paper by Best Book/Transcontinental Printing
Cover design: Susan Shapiro
Cover painting: © Christie's Images, Ltd. 1999
        "La Espera" (1948), by Hector Poleo

Some of these poems have been previously published in *Cedar Hill Review*
and *Gravitas, Inc.*

This book was published with the support of the Connecticut
Commission on the Arts, the National Endowment for the Arts and
donations from many individuals. We are very grateful for this support.

We are deeply grateful to Maya Flakoll Gross for her assistance with the
translation. We are also grateful to Jane Blanshard and Sonia Cintron
Marrero for their help in copy-editing this manuscript.

Library of Congress Cataloging-in-Publication Data

Alegría, Claribel.
        Sorrow / by Claribel Alegría ; translated by Carolyn Forché.
    — 1st ed.
            p. cm.
        Added title page title: Saudade.
        ISBN 1-880684-63-2 (paper)
        1. Alegría, Claribel. Translations into English. I. Forché, Carolyn.
    II. Title. III. Title: Saudade.
    PQ7539.A47S67 1999
    861—dc21   99-27585

published by
        CURBSTONE PRESS   321 Jackson Street   Willimantic, CT 06226
            phone: 860-423-5110   e-mail: info@curbstone.org
                            http://www.curbstone.org
                            Printed in Canada

A Bud,
que me precedió en el viaje.

To Bud,
who precedes me on the journey.

¿Adónde te escondiste
Amado, y me dejaste con gemido?
— San Juan de la Cruz

Where have you hidden,
Beloved, leaving me sobbing?
—St. John of the Cross

CONTENTS

Translator's Preface

The wind has arrived from the coast of North Africa, lemon-scented and gentle, but the beginning of a sirocco, the desert wind of sand and cries. We are sitting on the terrace of C'an Blau Vell, the house in Deya, Mallorca, where Claribel Alegría and her husband, Darwin "Bud" Flakoll, lived in self-imposed exile. This is a special evening: their daughters, Maya, Karen, and Patricia are here, along with the grandchildren. Robert Graves has walked down the hill on his wife Beryl's steadying arm. Someone brings out a bottle of Spanish wine, and then from the larder of the old stone house come ripe apricots, olives, and bread, little slivers of

fish and sliced lemon. We take turns reading poems and translations of poems aloud. The sun slips behind the peak of the Teix, and the copper-belled goats descend along the goat-paths. For a moment, it is possible to hear the *torrente* rushing along its rockbed below a wall of morning glories which are closed for the night.

We talk about the little towns of the Americas' isthmus, Estelí, Santa Ana, San Miguel, distant places suffering brutal poverty and dictatorship, and the land-scape of Claribel's childhood. But the wars which would bring about the fall of the Somoza dictatorship in Nicaragua and the end of military rule in El Salvador have not yet begun. The countries are "at peace," as yet, which is the silence of misery endured.

A wind passes through the olive trees and silvers them. Bud takes Claribel's hand and they look into each other's eyes for a long time. Over their heads, bougainvillea blossoms in the thirtieth summer of their marriage, and it is apparent to all of us that what had begun as a passionate, whirlwind three-month romance in 1947, had, over years of child-raising on the wing, uprootedness that brought them to live in Mexico, Uruguay, Chile, France and Spain, become an unusual union: spiritual, conjugal, dedicated to art and literature but also awake to human suffering, such that it would bless the world in the seventeen years to come, when Claribel and Bud would end their exile and begin a new, collaborative work: that of developing the testimonio as a distinct and necessary form.

The grandchildren have fallen asleep and the stars have appeared; Robert Graves has tipped his wide-brimmed hat and said goodnight. In an hour we will go inside "the old blue house" and listen to tangos on the phonograph; there will be laughter and stories, and we will be grateful for these, because they will lift Claribel's spirits, assuaging the sadness peculiar to life in exile.

This is the summer when her poetry would enter the English language for the first time. Despite my inexperience, I had undertaken to translate her *Flores del Volcán*, ("Flowers From the Volcano,") a volume recalling her childhood in Sihuatehuacán, "the valley of beautiful witches," a world dimly lit and suffering, scented with jasmine, in which the poor harvest flowers from the craters of dead volcanoes, and bear them in their arms down its slopes. It is a book of loss, and also a poignant *cri de cœur*, raging against the violence of political repression, written at a time when the dead have become "too many to bury," and her memory, a cemetery of her dead. Mornings I struggle to inhabit this lyric otherness, and to bear her music across the river of a new language without spilling too much. Her obsessions are with love and death, as they had always been, but also with the mystery of time, presence, otherness, and the evanescence of subjectivity. One of the most ambitious poems of the collection, titled in English "Sorrow," recounts her search for the grave of Spanish poet Federico García Lorca, and toward its closure she imagines herself imprisoned and writes: una hoja de tiempo, "only a tissue of time/a tissue separates us," the living from the dead. These lines seed a new exploration in her work, which will endure and flower in the present volume *Sorrow*, an awareness of the mysteries of temporality, particularly as it bears upon the separation of the living from the dead.

The summer night in Deya is long, starry, and our festivities end near dawn. Within a year, I will be in El Salvador, and within two, Claribel and Bud will leave Deya for Managua, Nicaragua, where they will research the history of the Sandinista revolution (*Nicaragua: La revolución sandinista,* Editorial ERA, 1982). Aside from for brief periods of rest and writing, they will never live in C'an Blau Vell again. Their son and grandson will live and work in Nicaragua, and the daughters will visit. I will meet my future husband, the American photographer Harry Mattison, in a refugee compound in El Salvador in 1980, and we will marry four years later. Bud will assume the work of translating Claribel's subsequent poetry books into English, and together they will write many testimonies. I will see him again only twice, once in the United States, and once when they visit us in Paris after the birth of our son.

In their last decade and a half together in Central America, Claribel and Bud dedicated themselves to a community of souls engaged in work on behalf of social justice. They were tireless and, by all reports and despite disappointments and hardships, filled with joy and unflagging in their devotion to each other. Toward what was to become the end of their time together, they planned to undertake a journey to southern Asia, quietly and for themselves. They had long planned to take this trip, along with their friends, Julio Cortázar and his wife, Carol Dunlop. Now both Julio and Carol were dead. Claribel and Bud dreamed and talked of the places they would visit, and of course, the spirits of Julio and Carol would accompany them. But Bud was by now himself ill, and after a long battle, died on April 15, 1995. A month later, Claribel left for Singapore, as she has said, along with the soul of her husband; together they traveled on the Orient Express, together walked the streets of Bangkok. Then they went by sea to Jakarta to visit the great and small temples of the Indonesian archipelago. Claribel whispered to Bud throughout the journey, describing what they were seeing together, the people they were meeting, the meals they took, the dreams in which they were once again together. After a month, she returned to Managua, and her posthumous dialogue with her husband entered her poems, those collected here in the book originally titled *Saudade*, a Portuguese word for a vague and persistent desire for something that cannot be, a time other than the present time, a turning toward the past or future, a sadness and yearning beyond sorrow, the pain which whispers through every happiness. It is the word which most corresponds in its intricacy of meaning to the profundity of intimate mourning at the loss of one's life companion.

In these poems, she resists her longing to join her beloved while somehow also preserving this longing. She resists the eternal transcendent, praising the most fleeting and fugitive of human moments. Exploring a more nuanced understanding of Ariadne's myth, as intertwining the sorrowful and celebratory aspects of marriage, she leaves her woolen thread for the beloved, but also becomes the one whose name "Very Holy," can be invoked at such epiphanic moments as the realization of the deceased beloved's continuing presence.

By turns she writes of Artemis, goddess of women's transitions, who empowers her in grief, and of Hermes, the messenger god whose winged sandals erase his own footprints, and who knows how to call upon the dead. Her Sisyphus reaches the summit without the burden of his boulder, but finds only "a pebble/a grain of sand." Her Icarus desires flight but also death: "I am coming/ the clouds are my tomb." Like Prometheus she is "tied to time/and cannot escape." She beseeches Orpheus for his song, his word "a lyre forged/with the cords/of my being" so that she may descend into the underworld in search of her beloved. Life becomes dream, and dreaming allows her to confuse sleep with death. In a series of poignant apostrophes, she addresses her other, the absent one, who speaks to her in turn, but in a language she doesn't always understand. Like Eugenio Montale of the *Mottetti*, her brief lyrics imagine world as oracle, as repository of the messages sent by those who are no longer. She tries to imagine their future reunion, as "particles of light" fusing or as wings folding together, but finally she refuses to settle for her beloved's absence, for his ghost, and desires their encounter to be corporeal: it is his body she longs for; his touch, his hands, and his absence become "a crow/gnawing at my entrails." She begins to contemplate the mysteries of metempsychosis, the soul's transmigration, or passage from one body to another. Knowledge of this is, finally, denied the living, and so she achieves her peace in the recognition that a triumph over sadness is possible.

She has, however, in *Sorrow,* constructed a sensibility in which time can be "rearranged," the past able to "cover" and "uncover" her. The concept of time begins to correspond with its fluidity and spatiality, as membrane between present and future, living and dead, permeable and illusionary. Always already setting out for the future, this poet's present is the point of departure and her passage is possible because she has "seized hold" of the beloved's light. There are echoes of Paul Celan ("death/that drinks me/and drinks me") in this transforming work of encountering otherness, as well as tributes to the long tradition of Spanish language love lyrics, but this poetry, is, finally, a work apart: a record of the passage of the human soul through searing grief and separation. "Happiness," she writes, "is a peach tree," and sadness, "a peach pecked by birds." Sadness is, therefore, the fruit of happiness, and can be in that sense nourishment. And there is also, in these poems, a knowledge of the power the living have on behalf of the dead: that of raising them up by our acts of remembrance.

I am grateful to Bud Flakoll for teaching me to hear Claribel Alegría's music, and to Claribel for inviting me back as translator following his death. This book is for all who have gone before and all who have remained behind to continue the journey.

—Carolyn Forché
June 19, 1999

SAUDADE
SORROW

Salí a buscarte

Salí a buscarte
atravesé valles
y montañas
surqué mares lejanos
le pregunté a las nubes
y al viento
inútil todo
inútil
dentro de mí estabas.

Searching for You

I went out searching for you
crossing valleys
and mountains
ploughing distant seas
asking of the clouds
and the wind your whereabouts
it was all useless
useless
you were within me.

Hoy es noche de sombras

Hoy es noche de sombras
de recuerdos-espada
la soledad me tumba.
Nadie que aguarde mi llegada
con un beso
y un ron
y mil preguntas.
La soledad retumba.
Quiere estallar de rabia
el corazón
pero le brotan alas.

This Is a Night of Shadows

This is a night of shadows
of sword-memories
solitude overwhelms me.
No one awaits my arrival
with a kiss
and a rum
and a thousand questions.
Solitude echoes within me.
My heart wishes
to burst with rage
but it sprouts wings.

Nostalgias II

Dejé de ser nosotros
y de nuevo este yo
con su carga de invierno
y de vacío.

Nostalgia II

I cease being us
and am again this I
with its burden of winter
and emptiness.

Lamentación de Ariadna

No te pierdas, Teseo
vuelve a mí.
La playa está desierta
tengo los pies sangrientos
de correr en tu busca.
¿Será que me engañaste
dejándome dormida en esta isla?
Perdóname, Teseo
¿Recuerdas nuestro encuentro?
Amor eterno me juraste
y yo te di el ovillo
y volviste a la luz
después de haber destruido
al minotauro.
¿Te secuestró algún dios
sintiéndose celoso?
No me inspiran temor
ni Poseidón
ni Zeus
es de fuego mi ira
y se alzará
desde estas aguas
hasta el cielo.
Vuelve,
vuelve, Teseo
no te pierdas
en los laberintos
de la muerte
anda suelto
el ovillo de mi amor
atrápalo, Teseo

The Lamentation of Ariadne

Don't lose yourself, Theseus
return to me.
The beach is deserted
I have bloody feet
from running in search of you.
Was it one of your tricks
to leave me asleep on this island?
Forgive me, Theseus
Do you recall how we met?
You swore eternal love
and I gave you the thread
and you returned to the light
after destroying
the minotaur.
Were you abducted by some
jealous God?
They do not inspire fear in me
neither Poseidon
nor Zeus
my wrath is fire
and will rise
from these waters
to the heavens.
Return,
return Theseus,
don't lose yourself
in the labyrinths
of death
go swiftly along
the thread of my love
seize it, Theseus

vuelve a mí
soy tu tierra
tu luna
tu destino.
Clava en mi tus raíces.

return to me
I am your earth
your moon
your destiny.
Sink your roots in me.

Casi al final

Casi al final de mi vida
y sigo sin entender.
Ni el amor
ni la muerte
he podido expresar.
Viví el amor contigo
contigo muero
el dolor de tu ausencia
ilumina a veces mi palabra.

Almost at the End

Almost at the end of my life
I still don't understand.
Neither love
nor death
have I been able to express.
I lived love with you
with you I die
sometimes the pain of your absence
illuminates my speech.

Figuraciones

Atravesé el espejo
pesqué del pelo al tiempo
y cabalgué con él
al otro lado.
Si regreso
se incrustrán en mí
los vidrios rotos
y en un tiempo sin tiempo
me hundiré.

Figurations

I passed through the mirror
took Time by the hair
and rode with him
to the other side.
If I return
broken glass
will encrust my flesh
and into a time without time
I will sink.

Hoy

Hoy se abrió tu camelia
y yo la gozo.
Con el agua se abrió
y será deshojada por el viento.

Today

Today your camellia opened
and I am enjoying it.
It opened with the rain
and the wind
will strip its leaves.

Insomnio

Digo amor
y lacera mi cuerpo
el desamparo.

Insomnia

I say love
and abandonment
lacerates my body.

Muero de a poco

Muero de a poco, amor
no es la muerte sorpresa
que deseaba
la que libera
y lanza
es la otra
la lenta
la que corta en pedazos
da estocadas
y de perfil se escurre.

Little by Little I Die

Little by little I die, my love
It's not the surprise death
I wanted
the one that frees
and launches
it's the other
the slow one
that cuts you into pieces
stabs you
and in profile steals away.

Saudade

Quisiera creer
que te veré otra vez
que nuestro amor
florecerá de nuevo
quizá seas un átomo de luz
quizá apenas existan tus cenizas
quizá vuelvas
y yo seré cenizas
un átomo de luz
o estaré lejana.
No volverá a repetirse
nuestro amor.

Sorrow

I wish I could believe
that I will see you again
that our love
will bloom again.
Perhaps you are an atom of light
perhaps your ashes barely exist
perhaps you will return
and I will be ash
an atom of light
or far away.
Our love
will never happen again.

Circe

Circe es mi nombre
me llaman bruja
y maga
y hechicera.
Amo el mar
la furia del mar
contra las rocas
y sus acantilados
tenebrosos.
Nunca amé a un mortal
ni siquiera a Ulises
pude amar.
Me gusta lo fugaz:
la chispa
y no la hoguera
el encuentro fortuito
sin adioses.
Fui siempre fiel a mi destino
me impulsaba
jugaba con los hombres
caían aturdidos
en mis redes
los convertía en bestias
los volvía a su forma
y seguían amándome
y tejían guirnaldas para mí.
Me cansé de mi juego
era pueril
los expulsé a todos
de una vez
me quedé sin esclavas
sin efebos

Circe

Circe is my name
they call me witch
and magician
and charmer.
I love the sea
the fury of the sea
against the rocks
and its dark cliffs.
I never loved a human
not even Ulysses
could I love.
I liked the fleeting moment
the spark
and not the blaze
the accidental encounter
without good-byes.
I was always faithful to my destiny
it propelled me.
I toyed with men
they fell giddy
into my nets.
I changed them into beasts
I changed them again into forms
and they went on loving me
and wove garlands for me.
I tired of my game
it was puerile.
I got rid of all of them
at once
I was left without slaves
without young men

sin bestias
sola
en mi isla sepulcral
yo sola frente al mar
con los alisios
condenada a mí misma
y a la paz.
Mis recuerdos son tersos
tengo dura y vacía
la mirada
mirada de gaviota
o de albatrós.
Quizá si hubiese amado
algún dardo heriría mi memoria.

without beasts
all alone
in my sepulchral island
all alone facing the sea
with the east winds
condemned to myself
and to peace.
My memories are terse
my gaze
hard and empty
the gaze of a sea gull
or albatross.
Perhaps if I had loved
some dart would pierce my memory.

Aunque te alejes, Muerte

No volveré a llamarte
aunque te alejes.
Te siento
no te veo
nunca he visto tu rostro
que me espía.
¿Eres hermosa,
fea?
Habitas donde habito
no puedo despegarme
de tu aliento.
Te escucho
no te oigo
no volveré a llamarte
aunque padezca.
Gozaré del momento
hasta que un día
de tu mano me escurra hacia la nada.

Even if You Go Away, Death

I will not call you back
even if you go away.
I feel you
I don't see you
never have I seen your face
spying on me.
Are you beautiful?
Ugly?
You live where I live
I can't escape your breath.
I hear you
but I don't listen
I will not call you back
even if it pains me.
I will enjoy the present moment
until one day
I will slip into nothingness holding your hand.

Para amarte de nuevo

Para amarte
de nuevo
fue preciso morir.

To Love You Again

To love you again
it was necessary to die.

Soy una gaviota

Soy una gaviota
solitaria
con el ala tronchada
abro un surco en la arena.

I Am a Sea Gull

I am a solitary sea gull
with my broken wing
digging a furrow in the sand.

Estás vivo

Estás vivo en mi pecho
y solo yo te siento.
Eres el alquimista
que transforma en poesía
nuestro llanto.

You Are Alive

You are alive in my breast
and only I can tell.
You are the alchemist
who transforms our cries into poetry.

Eres mi otro Yo

Eres mi otro yo
mi vagabundo yo
mi espejo-puente.
Convocando silencios
empiezo a comprender:
mi destino eres tú
y no sé qué hacer
contra tu muerte.
Día y noche
te busco
el tiempo que me sobra
lo distraigo
con preguntas
y lágrimas
y hastío.
Te busco en las auroras
en las sombras
en los vericuetos de mi yo
en la fosforescencia
del desvelo.
En mi herida te busco
en mi dolor
queriendo atravesarlo
rebasarlo
hasta llegar a ti.

You Are My Other I

You are my other I
my vagabond I
my mirror-bridge.
Convening silences
I begin to understand:
you are my destiny
and I don't know what to do
against your death.
Day and night
I search for you
I distract time
with questions
and tears
and boredom.
I search for you in my daybreaks
among the shadows
in the wilderness of my I
in the phosphorescence
of vigilance.
I search for you in my wound
in my sorrow
wishing to pierce it
to overflow it
until I reach you.

Todo me habla de muerte

Todo me habla de muerte:
esa flor que se abre
tus pupilas
el pájaro que cruza
la marea
el ocaso.
¿Por qué pide nacer
este poema?

Everything Speaks of Death

Everything speaks to me of death
the flower opening
the bird moving across
the tide
the sunset.
Why does this poem
ask to be born?

No quiero

No quiero ser eterna
la eternidad me abruma
quiero estar viva
mientras viva
sin pensar
por qué
vivo
ser un relámpago en el aire
una mariposa iridescente
un pasajera pompa de jabón.

I Don't Want Eternity

I don't want eternity
it overwhelms me
I want to be alive
while I live
without thinking
about why
I live
I want to be lightning
in the air
an iridescent butterfly
a soap bubble about to burst.

Dame tu mano

"Hoy me gusta la vida mucho menos
pero siempre me gusta vivir"
—César Vallejo

Dame tu mano
amor
no dejes que me hunda
en la tristeza
Ya mi cuerpo aprendió
el dolor de tu ausencia
y a pesar de los golpes
quiere seguir viviendo.
No te alejes
amor
encuéntrame en el sueño
defiende tu memoria
mi memoria de ti
que no quiero extraviar.
Somos la voz
y el eco
el espejo y el rostro
dame tu mano
espera
debo ajustar mi tiempo
hasta alcanzarte.

Give Me Your Hand

"Today I like life much less
but I always like living"
                —César Vallejo

Give me your hand
my love
don't let me sink
into sadness.
My body has already learned
the grief of your absence
but despite the blows
it still wants to live.
Don't go away
love
meet me in my dreams
defend your memory
my memory of you
that I don't want to lose.
We are voice and echo
mirror
and face
give me your hand
wait
I have to rearrange my time
until I reach you.

Invitación

No sé qué mares
ríos
o secretos pasajes
tendrás que atravesar
pero te espero hoy
hacia el ocaso
a que escuchemos juntos
una fuga de Bach.

Invitation

I don't know what seas
rivers
or secret passages
you have to cross
but I'm waiting for you today
at sunset
so we may listen together
to a Bach fugue.

¿Cómo será el encuentro?

¿Cómo será el encuentro?
Descarnados los dos
sin tu mirada
sin mis labios
posándose en los tuyos.
Partículas de luz quizá seremos
que se atraen
se buscan
se amalgaman.

What Will Our Meeting Be Like?

What will our meeting be like?
Both of us without bodies
without your gaze
without my lips
on yours.
Perhaps we will be
particles of light
attracting each other
searching for each other
and finally fusing.

No estoy sola

No estoy sola
ni lo estaré jamás
me acompaña tu ausencia.

I Am Not Alone

I am not alone
and never will be
your absence is my company.

El pasado me cubre

El pasado me cubre
me descubre
es en mi cuerpo un manto
pletórico de signos
de señales.
En cada gesto mío
en cada giro
otro gesto anterior que me confirma
y me lanza al futuro.

My Past Covers Me

My past covers me
uncovers me
it is a mantle over my body
filled with signs
with signals.
In each of my gestures
in each turn
another gesture
confirms me
and launches me into the future.

Me gusta elaborar
mis pensamientos

Me gusta elaborar
mis pensamientos
los manipulo un rato
los esculpo
para soltarlos luego
y verlos agitarse
ante mis ojos.

I Like to Elaborate
My Thoughts

I like to elaborate
my thoughts
manipulate them for a while
sculpt them
set them free
and see them tremble
before my eyes.

¿Y si me muero y sueño?

¿Y si me duermo y sueño que estoy muerta
y en realidad he muerto
y no lo sé
y despierto a una luz
que no es la mía
a un paisaje ignoto
que me ignora
¿lucharé por volver
a mi apacible espacio
pensándome atrapada
en una pesadilla
o en un instante luz
sabré que estoy despierta
que al fin he despertado
del sueño de la vida?

And if I Die and Dream?

And if I fall asleep and dream that I am dead
and in fact have died
and don't know it
and I awaken to a light
that is not mine
to an unknown land
that ignores me
would I fight to go back
to my peaceful place
thinking I am trapped
in a nightmare
or in a light-instant
will I know I am awake
that at last I have awakened
from life's dream?

Aferrada

Aferrada a tu luz
atravieso mi tiempo
ha habido y habrá
inesperados vientos
huracanes
tormentas
y sequías,
pero sé desde siempre
que tú me sostendrás.

Seizing Hold

Seizing your light
I pass through time
there have been and will be
unexpected winds
hurricanes
storms
and droughts
but I have always known
that you'll hold on to me.

Te invento

Te invento en el jardín
invento que me hablas
que me llamas
y en realidad me hablas
y a veces no comprendo
lo que dices
y me asombro de ti
de tu misterio
y finjo que comprendo
para que no te alejes.
Día a día te invento
y esa es mi manera
de enfrentarme a tu ausencia
porque de no inventarte
se esfumaría el gozo
de mis horas
y tú te esfumarías.

I Invent You

I invent you in the garden
I invent that you talk to me
that you call me
and in fact you do talk to me
and sometimes I don't understand
what you say
and I am amazed at you
at your mystery
and I pretend that I understand
so that you won't go away.
Day after day I invent you
and that's my way
of confronting your absence
because if I don't invent you
the joy of my hours
would vanish
and you as well.

Invocación a la Muerte

No ya el desasosiego
pero sí el deseo
la esperanza
de encontrarte a la vuelta de la esquina
para cortar de un tajo
el hilo que me clava.

Invocation to Death

No longer the restlessness
but the desire
the hope
to encounter you turning the corner
so as to break the rivet
that fastens me.

Mi laberinto

Mi laberinto es circular
voy cavando en el aire
con los ojos clavados
en la muerte
que me bebe
y me bebe
en cada vuelta.

My Labyrinth

My labyrinth is circular
I go digging in the air
with my eyes fixed
on death
that drinks me
and drinks me
at every turn.

Artemisa

Eres la triple diosa
la triple diosa luna
que engendra en mí
visiones.
Disparas desde lejos
y asciendo
y desciendo
me llevas de la luz
a las tinieblas
y otra vez a la luz
y al terror.
Eres la madre buena
la de múltiples pechos
que nutre todo lo que vive
la virgen cazadora
queriendo atravesar el horizonte
la voraz taladora
la fuerza que me arrastra
y me transforma.
Nuestro vuelo es nocturno
y volamos
volamos
Artemisa
y yo bebo tu leche
y cruzamos galaxias
y amamanto serpientes
en mi vuelo
y acuno a la muerte
entre mis pechos
y la muerte está viva
resplandece
y sigo el vuelo de tu flecha

Artemis

You are the triple goddess
the triple moon goddess
who engenders
visions in me.
From far off you shoot
and I ascend
and descend
you carry me from light
into shadows
and again toward light
and toward terror.
You are the good mother
the one with multiple breasts
who nurtures everything alive
the hunter virgin
who wants to cross the horizon
the voracious destroyer
the force that leads
and transforms me.
Our flight is nocturnal
and we fly and we fly
Artemis
and I drink your milk
and we cross galaxies
and I nurse serpents
in my flight
and I cradle death
between my breasts
and death is alive
it shines
and I follow the flight of your arrow

y te pierdo
Artemisa
y desciendo al abismo
y la muerte se encoge
y se me vuelve momia
y estoy aquí de nuevo
con los ojos abiertos
vieron su oscuridad
en las estrellas
y no quieren cerrarse
y hay en ellos tierra
y hay polvo estelar.
Ayúdame
Artemisa
los párpados me pesan:
una canción de cuna
o tu certera flecha.

and I lose you
Artemis
and I descend into the abyss
and death shrinks
and becomes a mummy
and I am here again
with my eyes open
that saw darkness
in the stars
and they don't want to close
and there is earth in them
and there is stellar dust.
Help me, Artemis
my eyelids weigh upon me:
a cradle song
or your sure arrow.

Rito incumplido

A mi madre

Dicen que la muerte es solitaria
que nos morimos solos
aunque estemos rodeados de aquellos que nos aman
pero tú me llamaste
y yo no estuve:
no te cerré los ojos
no te besé la frente
no te ayudé a pasar
al otro lado
estuve lejos
lejos de ti que me alumbraste
me nutriste
educaste mis alas.
No cumplí con el rito
estuve lejos
lejos
y ese es el sollozo que me arrebata en olas
en cúpulas
en grutas
y no puede salir
y me persigue en sueños
y me ahoga.
Perdóname/libérame
necesito aullar
batir tambores
un golpe en la cerviz
un estallido
para arrancar de cuajo este sollozo
y no invocarte más
en desolados
versos.

Unfinished Rite

to my mother

They say death is a solitary thing
that we die alone
though surrounded by those who love us,
but you called out to me
and I was not there:
I didn't close your eyes,
I didn't kiss your brow,
I didn't help you cross
over to the other side:
I was far away
far from you who gave me birth
who nourished me
who trained my wings for flight.
I didn't fulfill the rite
I was far away
too far
and that is the sob that carries me off in waves
in domes
in caves
and can't escape
and follows me around in dreams
and smothers me.
Forgive me/free me
for I need
to howl, beat drums
I need a blow to the nape of my neck
an explosion
to rip this sob out of me
So I no longer need to call upon you
in these my desolate
verses.

Alegría

Alegría:
Un durazno
en todo su esplendor.

Happiness

Happiness:
a peach
in all its splendor

Tristeza

Tristeza:
Un durazno
picoteado por pájaros

Sadness

Sadness:
a peach
pecked by birds.

Hermes

Te llevo prisionero
en un anillo
tus sandalias aladas
me arrebatan
eres lira en mis manos
luz de sombra
buceo en mis abismos
con tu luz
y encuentro desiertos
sirenas extraviadas
que sollozan
pero hay también infancia
crepúsculos con playas
y ternura.
Vas marcando mis pasos
escribo enfebrecida
buceo en el pasado
en el presente
y pierdo el equilibrio
y caigo
y caigo.
No me hagas profecías
no las quiero
no quiero que se anclen
mis sentidos.
Necesito tu hoz
para cortar instantes
para talar cosas imposibles:
alfabetos
y músicas
y sueños
y hacerlos brillar

Hermes

I carry you as a prisoner
in my ring
your winged sandals
bear me away
you are a lyre in my hands
shadow's light
I dive into my abysses
with your light
and I encounter deserts
lost sirens
weeping
but there are also childhood
sunsets on beaches
and tenderness.
You mark my footsteps
I write feverishly
I dive into the past
into the present
and I lose my balance
and I fall
and I fall.
Don't make prophecies
I don't want them
I don't want my senses
anchored.
I need your scythe
to cut moments
to cut impossible things
alphabets
and music
and dreams
and make them shine

en mi penumbra.
Te llevo prisionero
en un anillo
pero eres tú
quien me fustiga.

in my twilight.
I carry you as a prisoner in my ring
but it's you who cudgels me.

Sísifo

Subo la cuesta
asciendo
avizoro la cumbre
un guijarro
un granito de arena
y resbalo otra vez
hasta el comienzo.

Sisyphus

I climb the slope
I ascend
I search the summit
a pebble
a grain of sand
and I slide once again
toward the beginning.

Metempsicosis

Si hay regreso
mi tiempo ha sido largo
si no lo hubiese
apenas un relámpago
furtivo.

Metempsychosis

If there is a return
my wait has been long
and if there is not
it has been barely
a sudden lightning flash.

Eres mío silencio

Ahora sí,
ya en el último umbral
eres mío
silencio.
Cuando fui quinceañera te inventé
saltando como un río
y la luz de tus aguas
me turbó.
Ahora
en mi vejez
ni te invento
ni te llamo
ni me turbas.
Eres parte de mí
de mí provienes
me pueblas con tus voces
te pueblo con las mías.
Me libero de ti
contigo mismo.

You Are Mine, Silence

Now
on my final threshold
you are mine, silence.
At fifteen I invented you
surging like a river
and the light on your water
confused me.
Now
in my old age
I neither invent you
nor call you
and you don't confuse me.
You are part of me
born in me
you people me with your voices
I people you with mine.
I free myself of you
and yet go with you.

No importa si en Yakarta

No importa si en Yakarta
en París
o en Umbría
el espejo me habla
en español.

It Doesn't Matter if in Jakarta

It doesn't matter if in Jakarta
or Paris
or in Umbria
the mirror speaks to me
in Spanish

Ultimo umbral

Un paso más
dos o tres quizá
un mirar hacia atrás
el vértigo
el abismo
y cruzar el umbral
que me lleve hacia ti.

Last Threshold

One more step
two or three perhaps
a look back
the vertigo
the abyss
and across the threshold
that takes me to you.

Reflexiones de Icaro

Son de cera mis alas
pero vuelo
y seguiré volando
aunque el sol las derrita
y me desplome.
No quisiera ser rey
de tierras desoladas
sin árboles
sin ríos
sin manos que abran puertas.
A través de sus lágrimas
me contempla mi padre
quizá me llamen loco
temerario
poeta
mas seguiré volando
alzándome hacia el sol
estoy llorando ahora
no quiero ver más cuervos
ni escuchar sus graznidos
se está encogiendo el mar
se borra el horizonte
me acerco
estoy llegando
las nubes son mi tumba.

The Reflections of Icarus

My wings are of wax
but I fly
and I'll go on flying
even if the sun melts them
and I plummet.
I wouldn't like to be king
of desolate lands
without trees
without rivers
without hands opening doors.
My father studies me
through his tears.
Perhaps they'll call me crazy
reckless
a poet
but I'll go on flying
rising toward the sun
I am crying now
I don't want to see more crows
I don't want to hear their cawing
the sea is shrinking
the horizon vanishes.
I am near
I am coming
the clouds are my tomb.

Nunca más

Nunca más
contemplaré contigo
el ocaso cereza
ni escucharemos
con manos enlazadas
un solo de Artie Shaw
nunca más
el calor de tus labios
en los míos
ni el sueño y el ensueño
compartidos.
Sin embargo es ahora
sólo ahora
después de tu partida
sin retorno
que sé que ya eres mío
para siempre.

Never Again

Never again
will I contemplate with you
the scarlet sunset
nor will we listen
hands entwined
to an Artie Shaw solo
never again
will the warmth of your lips
touch mine
nor will we share
our dreams and fantasies.
It is now
and only now
since your voyage of no return
that I know you are mine
forever.

Cada vez

Cada vez
que los nombro
resucitan mis muertos.

Every Time

Every time I name them
my dead are resurrected.

Prometeo

A ti, a ti te quiero.
—Dora Guerra T.

No quiero vivir con tu fantasma
a ti
a ti te quiero
a la luz de tus ojos
en los míos
a tus labios nombrándome
besándome
al sabor de tu piel
al olor de tu cuerpo
a tus dedos enredándose
en mi pelo
a tus pasos señalándome
el camino.
No quiero adivinarte
en una nube
ni acecharte en el sueño
ni masticar memorias
ya marchitas.
A ti
a ti te quiero
a tus ojos
a tus labios
a tus manos
es un cuervo tu ausencia
que me roe
y estoy atada al tiempo
y no puedo escapar.

Prometheus

It's you, it's you whom I love.
—Dora Guerra T

I don't want to live with your ghost
it's you
you I love
the light in your eyes
in mine
your lips naming me
kissing me
the taste of your skin
the smell of your body
your fingers entwined
in my hair
your footsteps
showing me the way.
I don't want to imagine you
in a cloud
or wait for you in my dreams
or chew on faded memories.
It's you
you I love
your eyes
your lips
your hands.
Your absence is a crow
gnawing my entrails
and I am tied to time
and cannot escape.

Abandoné mis máscaras

Abandoné mis máscaras
y vuelvo a ser yo misma
vulnerable.
Apenas sé quién soy
no hay lazos que me aten
al amor
al deber
a la jóven que fui
o a la muerte que aguarda.
Estoy a la deriva
sólo importa este instante
este presente
mi realidad huidiza
que me arrastra
y se transforma en otra
y me transforma
y la noche es la misma
y no te encuentro.

I Gave Up My Masks

I gave up my masks
and I am myself again
vulnerable.
I hardly know who I am
there are no ties
to love
to duty
to the young girl I was
to death that awaits me.
I am adrift
only this moment counts
this present
my slippery reality
that leads me
and transforms itself into another
and transforms me
and the night is the same
and I cannot find you.

Dos alas en el vuelo

Fuimos una incauta
mariposa
dos alas en el vuelo
que se volvían una
en el reposo.

Two Wings in Flight

We were a careless
butterfly
two wings in flight
that folded into one
in repose.

Orfeo

Dame tu canto
Orfeo
tu palabra
una lira forjada
con las cuerdas
de mi ser.
Debo descender
al reino de los muertos
despertar a mi amado
y hechizarlo.

Orpheus

Give me your song
Orpheus
your word
a lyre forged
with the cords
of my being.
I must descend
to the kingdom of the dead
and awaken my beloved
and bewitch him.

No puede

No puede conmigo
la tristeza
la arrastro hacia la vida
y se evapora.

It Cannot

Sadness
can't cope with me
I lead it toward life
and it evaporates.

CURBSTONE PRESS, INC.

is a non-profit publishing house dedicated to literature that reflects a commitment to social change, with an emphasis on contemporary writing from Latino, Latin American, and Vietnamese cultures. Curbstone presents writers who give voice to the unheard in a language that goes beyond denunciation to celebrate, honor, and teach. Curbstone builds bridges between its writers and the public – from inner-city to rural areas, colleges to community centers, children to adults. Curbstone seeks out the highest aesthetic expression of the dedication to human rights and intercultural understanding: poetry, testimonies, novels, stories, and children's books.

This mission requires ensuring that as many people as possible know about these books and read them. To achieve this, a large portion of Curbstone's schedule is dedicated to arranging tours and programs for its authors, working with public school and university teachers to enrich curricula, reaching out to underserved audiences by donating books and conducting readings and community programs, and promoting discussion in the media. It is only through these combined efforts that literature can truly make a difference.

Curbstone Press, like all non-profit presses, depends on the support of individuals, foundations, and government agencies to bring you, the reader, works of literary merit and social significance which might not find a place in commercial publishing channels, and to bring the authors and their books into communities across the country. Our sincere thanks to the many individuals who support this endeavor and to the following businesses, foundations, and government agencies: Josef and Anni Albers Foundation, Connecticut Commission on the Arts, Connecticut Arts Endowment Fund, Connecticut Humanities Council, Lannan Foundation, Lawson Valentine Foundation, National Endowment for the Arts, Open Society Institute, Puffin Foundation, and the Edward C. & Ann T. Roberts Foundation.

Please support Curbstone's efforts to present the diverse voices and views that make our culture richer. Tax-deductible donations can be made by check or credit card to:
Curbstone Press, 321 Jackson Street, Willimantic, CT 06226
phone: (860) 423-5110   fax: (860) 423-9242   www.curbstone.org

IF YOU WOULD LIKE TO BE A MAJOR SPONSOR OF A CURBSTONE BOOK, PLEASE CONTACT US.